Original title:
Blooming Rhymes

Copyright © 2025 Creative Arts Management OÜ
All rights reserved.

Author: Victor Mercer
ISBN HARDBACK: 978-1-80566-630-1
ISBN PAPERBACK: 978-1-80566-915-9

Nature's Rhyme Scheme

The daisies wear their sunny hats,
While squirrels dance like acrobats.
Bees buzz tunes in perfect time,
While frogs compose a croaky mime.

The trees sway gently in the breeze,
Tickling leaves as if to tease.
A butterfly flutters without a care,
Joking with flowers that bloom everywhere.

The Cadence of Clovers

Clover patches hide silly gnomes,
Who laugh and sing like garden foams.
With jaunty hats and tiny shoes,
Creating chaos in grassy hues.

When raindrops fall, they bounce around,
Turning puddles into merry ground.
A stuck-up snail plays king of the hill,
While bumblebees dance with carefree thrill.

The Harmonics of Hyacinths

Hyacinths waltz in pots divine,
Chattering flowers in a vine.
A mischievous matchstick mouse,
Hums along inside his house.

Ladybugs wear polka dot suits,
While grasshoppers strum tiny flutes.
The clouds join in with a puffy beat,
Jiving together where the sun and sky meet.

Timeless Tangles

In tangled vines and playful sprigs,
A tangle of tales from nature digs.
Wiggly worms groove in the ground,
As worms in a conga line abound.

Cactuses flex their prickly spines,
Sporting shades of bright designs.
Laughter echoes in leafy groves,
Nature bleeds humor as it behoves.

Verses Under the Moonlight

A mushroom danced across the floor,
It wiggled, jiggled, then it swore.
The stars above began to blink,
And called the owl to share a drink.

The moon chuckled at the sight,
As lettuce wore a hat so tight.
A carrot played the ukulele,
And all the peas sang out, 'Hurray!'

Nature's Rhythmic Symphony

The squirrels form a funky band,
With acorns used as cymbals planned.
Bees buzz in perfect harmony,
While flowers sway, a sight to see.

A fox in shades joins in the fun,
As mushrooms glow like tiny suns.
The breeze is acting like a DJ,
Turning leaves into a ballet!

The Poetry of Sunflowers

Sunflowers make the silliest face,
They challenge roses to a race.
With heads held high, they start to tease,
And giggle when the wind's a breeze.

The daisies join, they wink and grin,
As bunnies hop and join the din.
Together they create such cheer,
Look out, world, the flowers are here!

Blossoms in the Breeze

A cactus tried to tell a joke,
But all it got was laughter and smoke.
A dandelion puffed and sighed,
'At least I'm not a cactus, right?'

The tulips burst into a song,
While petals fluttered all along.
They danced and twirled, a merry show,
In gardens where the wild winds blow.

Rhymes at Twilight's Edge

Beneath the moon, my socks do dance,
In mismatched pairs, they take a chance.
The crickets sing a silly tune,
While fireflies jiggle under the moon.

A cat in shades, looking so fine,
Sips from a cup of herbal wine.
The stars, they laugh at our delight,
As we twirl around in the soft twilight.

A Symphony of New Beginnings

The toaster popped, my bagel flew,
I ducked and dodged, oh who knew?
My coffee spilled, it made a splash,
At breakfast time, we're quite the clash!

A parrot sings out, 'Do it again!'
I giggle loud; it's my best friend.
We start the day with jokes in hand,
And toast our laughs, oh isn't it grand?

Petals Whisper

A sunflower's hat is quite the sight,
It waves and dances with pure delight.
The daisies gossip, oh what a chat,
'Look at that bee, he's got a big hat!'

The roses blush, all red and shy,
As dandelions float gently by.
They share their tales, both wild and fun,
In this garden party under the sun.

Verses in the Garden

In the garden, the veggies joke,
A carrot cracked up, then nearly broke.
'Tomatoes blush when they hear a pun,'
They giggle round the patch, oh what fun!

The radish teases, 'I'm rootin' for peas!'
While zucchinis sway lightly in the breeze.
They laugh and play all day till dark,
In this wacky garden, let's make our mark!

Pollen and Prose

In the garden, bees take flight,
Sneezing flowers, what a sight!
Petals dance on breezy days,
Honey drips in golden ways.

Worms in hats, they wiggle 'round,
Waving to the grass, so proud!
Daisies giggle at the sun,
Saying, "Time for lots of fun!"

Ode to the Blooming World

Tulips bounce in vibrant cheer,
Shouting, "Spring is finally here!"
Laughter echoes, daisies sway,
Pansies join the playful fray.

Butterflies wear polka dot ties,
"Who wore it best?"—a grand surprise!
Nature's jokes, a quirk or two,
Makes us smile, it's all true!

Lyrics from the Leafy Canopy

Squirrels sing in treetop bands,
Twirling nuts like disco plans!
Leaves are clapping, roots tap dance,
Nature's groove, a silly chance.

Caterpillars on the prowl,
Practicing their coolest howl.
"Who's the best?" they jokingly tease,
Strutting 'neath the swaying trees.

The Verse of Daybreak

Morning sun, a golden tease,
Waking flowers, little breeze.
Chirping birds with jokes to share,
Nature's laughter fills the air.

Roses blush, they can't deny,
Tickled by a butterfly.
Sunflowers stand, they take a bow,
"To sunny days, we all say wow!"

Sonnet of the Santan

In gardens bright, a flower stands proud,
Red like the sun, it laughs loud.
With petals wide, it waves its hand,
A joke on bees, all part of the plan.

The neighbors frown, their flowers so plain,
While Santan grins through sun or rain.
"I'm the star!" it seems to declare,
As butterflies dance in the warm air.

The lawnmower rolls, but it won't dare,
To mess with this diva giving flair.
Its roots hold secrets, you wouldn't believe,
Of parties and pranks that it weaves.

Oh, Santan, queen of this green parade,
With each giggle, your colors invade.
We laugh along at your vibrant spree,
In this garden stage, forever free.

Elysium in Bloom

In a village of petals, the laughter erupts,
The flowers wear glasses, oh how they look up!
A daisy plays chess with a sneaky coneflower,
While tulips debate the best dance hour.

The lilacs are gossiping, sharing their tea,
About the shy violets, who just want to be.
Each stem has a tale that they can confide,
In this quirky botanical joyride.

There's a rose with a quip that's sharp as a thorn,
Yet its sweet perfume leaves us all quite worn.
Peonies prance with their ruffled attire,
While sunflowers grinning aspire to higher.

So here in this realm where whimsy awakes,
Every bud knows the fun that it makes.
In this circus of color, we twirl and we cheer,
For laughter grows wild, and it's always near.

Celestial Stems

In the garden, stars take root,
With twinkling leaves that dance and shoot.
A daisy wears a comical hat,
While lilies giggle, chasing the cat.

Sunflowers swear they can touch the sky,
But when they jump, they just pass by.
Tulips tell jokes, and bees can't stop,
From buzzing along, right to the top.

Carrots confuse their friends at night,
Claiming they too can get a flight.
With twirling roots, they strut with glee,
While radishes laugh in harmony.

So watch the blooms, with smiles so wide,
In the garden where funny things hide.
A place where laughter grows on each stem,
And petals crack jokes, like they're in a gem.

Interval of Irises

Irises dance in a quirky tune,
Playing hopscotch 'neath the moon.
Each petal tells a silly tale,
Of frogs that wear huge shoes to scale.

Gardens hosting a game of charades,
Where sunbeams serve as jovial blades.
Petunias scribble jokes in the air,
While daisies wiggle without a care.

The violets cheer at every play,
Making mischief the whole day.
A comedy show that never ends,
With giggles shared among all friends.

So come and join this floral fare,
In a world where laughter fills the air.
With irises leading a funny spree,
In the colorful realm of comedy.

Whispers of Wildflowers

Wildflowers whisper their secrets low,
As butterflies plot a grand show.
With giggles and glee, they prance on by,
Chasing each other under the sky.

A poppy tells tales of snoozing bees,
Who wear pajamas and dance with ease.
Dandelions blow wishes that laugh,
While clovers giggle at their own path.

The daisies tease the bees for a ride,
Claiming their nectar's the best, with pride.
And ferns drape themselves in charmed delight,
As thistles express their wild thoughts bright.

In this patch of color and jest galore,
Funny moments bloom forever more.
With whispers shared in every hue,
A wildflower's laughter is always true.

The Melodic Meadow

In the meadow, melodies play,
Where flowers sing and bees sway.
Choruses of color ring so clear,
With humor that's hard to endear.

A spinning daffodil on a hill,
Thought it could dance, but lacks the skill.
But who needs rhythm in the sun?
When every petal's having fun!

Pansies hum a cheerful tune,
While cranky cacti grump 'neath the moon.
Tulips twist to an offbeat song,
In the meadow where all belong.

So let's join this garden of glee,
With laughter as fresh as the sea.
In this melodic place, spirits soar,
Where every bloom whispers more and more.

Echoes of Springtime

A duck in a hat sings a tune,
As flowers giggle beneath the moon.
Worms in shades of violet and green,
Dance like they're on a big screen.

Bumblebees buzzing with style so fine,
They land on a daisy, sip nectar like wine.
The tulips twirl in a jolly parade,
While the sun's rays play charades in the shade.

Squirrels in suits, what a sight to see,
Debating on branches, as wise as can be.
Nature's a circus, under the sky,
With laughter and joy, oh me, oh my!

Daffodils chuckle, the trees join the jest,
While frogs swap tales, having a fest.
What silly antics, oh, what a scene,
In this whimsical play, where no one's mean!

Nature's Poetic Palette

In a field of crayons, nature's array,
The daisies paint smiles, come what may.
A butterfly chuckles, flutters with flair,
In the center of flowers, without a care.

Sprouts in striped socks, oh what a sight,
Tickle the daisies, feeling just right.
Skunks in shades of navy and red,
Whisper sweet nothings, tucked in their bed.

Caterpillars crafting a wiggly dance,
On a twinkling leaf, they take a chance.
A rabbit with glasses reads under a tree,
Enjoying a pun, as funny as can be!

Nature's a canvas, wild and bright,
Where laughter erupts, a pure delight.
So grab a brush, let's splash and play,
Join in the fun, come what may!

Blossom and Rhyme

The florals are singing a silly song,
Bouncing with giggles, they all sing along.
Bees have their chorale, buzzing with glee,
While daisies are tap-dancing, oh can't you see?

Roses wear capes, oh they're feeling grand,
Playing hide-and-seek in the tall grass stand.
Butterflies flutter, a colorful spree,
Like confetti in the air, wild and free!

The grasshoppers tendo a 'stomp' of delight,
Making up rhythms under moonlight.
Ants march in file, with a comical style,
Laughing as they do, they'll travel a mile!

In this fiesta of petals and rhyme,
Nature's a jester, having good time.
With chuckles and cheer, till the day passes by,
Nature's a playground, beneath the blue sky!

Stanzas of the Wild

The trees sing odes in a raucous tone,
While squirrels write tales of twins they've shown.
A creek hums a ballad, bubbling with cheer,
As frogs serenade, "Come join us, my dear!"

Lizards in hats throw epic soirées,
Inviting all critters to dance and to play.
The bushes all giggle, tickled with sass,
As petals sway gently, wearing their grass.

Rabbits tell myths of the carrot affair,
While ladybugs promise to always be fair.
Nature's an artist, in coats of bright hue,
We'll scribble our stories, me and you!

So let's raise our voices, in this playful spree,
In stanzas of wild, oh be you and be me!
A laughter-filled party beneath the bright skies,
Where joy flies like confetti, oh how it does rise!

Hues of Hope

A daffodil wore a hat, quite proud,
Said, 'I'm the best, I'm blooming loud!'
But tulips chuckled, laughing hard,
'In spring's parade, you're just a card!'

The daisies danced in summer's breeze,
While sunflowers swayed, saying 'Please!'
They painted fields in yellow bright,
Making even snails take flight!

The roses blushed, they simply pruned,
Gossiping 'What's with that balloon?'
A bee buzzed past, he wore a grin,
Said, 'Let the pollinating begin!'

As colors flashed, the sky turned blue,
Each petal's laugh, a joyful hue.
Nature's canvas, so upbeat,
With silly blooms to tiptoe on feet!

A Palette of Pollen

The bumblebee wore a little tie,
He buzzed around with a wink and a sigh.
'Got pollen on my shoe,' he would say,
'Got to pollinate before I play!'

The lilacs laughed, their fragrance sweet,
'Careful, don't trip on our dainty feet!'
They painted gardens with shades of cheer,
While butterflies added, 'We're all here!'

A peony threw a wild flower bash,
And all the blooms joined in with a splash.
But a cactus pricked all with his grin,
'Come on in, let the fun begin!'

With petals spinning round and round,
A vibrant laugh is what they found.
Brushes dipped in joy's delight,
Painting gardens from morning to night!

The Sway of the Stem

The stems began their wiggly dance,
With leafy partners, they took a chance.
The tulips twirled, their heads held high,
While violets giggled, saying 'Oh my!'

Grass blades formed a little line,
'In this grand show, we all will shine!'
They jiggled and wobbled in the sun,
With rhythmic rustles, oh, what fun!

In the meadow, a butterfly played,
Stole the spotlight—unafraid!
He flapped and flirted, causing a stir,
All the blooms began to purr!

So if you see them sway and bend,
Join the fun, let laughter blend.
Nature's stage, a merry aspect,
With silly smiles that one shouldn't neglect!

Flourishing Words

The daisies gathered, a book club team,
Gossiping 'bout the latest dream.
A sunflower asked, 'What's on the page?'
'How to grow big, and take center stage!'

A dandelion blurted, 'Don't be so stiff!'
'Just blow in the wind, be free, take a lift!'
They cracked jokes about growing tall,
Saying, 'Who needs a fence, we'll just stall!'

As petals shared their wildest charms,
The garden echoed with all their psalms.
With laughter bubbling, they turned the leaves,
In nature's book, it's fun that we weave.

So here's to the blooms that wink and sway,
In rhymes and giggles, we'll spend our day.
Let words take flight on this green parade,
In the garden of joy, let's never fade!

Symphony of Sprouts

In a garden full of green,
The sprouts are quite a scene.
They wiggle, dance, and twirl,
In their own leafy whirl.

Singing songs of photosynthesis,
With all the joy that it gives us.
They tickle bugs, they tease the bees,
Growing up with goofy ease.

With a wink and a little grin,
They pop up, fun begins!
Chasing shadows, soaking sun,
Making gardening pure fun.

Their giggles spill with every shoot,
Shaking off the dirt, oh what a hoot!
A symphony of life's delight,
Sprouting joy both day and night.

The Chorus of Cherry Blossoms

In springtime's gentle air,
Cherry blossoms dance with flair.
Their petals twirl like ballerinas,
A sight that truly wins arenas.

They laugh, they sway in vibrant hue,
Tickling noses, oh so true.
With every breeze, they take a bow,
Nature's show, here and now.

With pink confetti in the sky,
They whisper secrets as they fly.
A chorus sings, oh what a riot,
Blossoms know how to start a quiet riot.

The bees are buzzing, oh what fun,
Join the dance, just run and run.
A celebration, springtime's treat,
With every petal, find your beat!

Softly Spoken Stems

In the quiet of the night,
Softly stems whisper delight.
They tell tales of sun and rain,
Of giggles caught in nature's brain.

With dew drops glistening like stars,
They recite their funny memoirs.
A little bent, a little shy,
They jive with each breeze that passes by.

Up and down, they sway and jest,
In their leafy caps, they dress the best.
They bow for bugs, and laugh for air,
Creating giggles everywhere.

Oh, the stories they could share,
Of tangled roots and bug affairs.
These softly spoken tales unwind,
In every nook, joy you will find.

Euphony of Earth

Deep in the soil, life starts to hum,
With every worm, a joyful strum.
Tiny roots play a merry tune,
Beneath the sun and the smile of the moon.

The earthworms squirm, they're quite the band,
With little critters lending a hand.
Together they dance and spin about,
Creating laughter, no room for doubt.

Fungi clap with their fluffy hats,
As dandelions play tag with bats.
While the daisies hum a catchy rhyme,
All life's creatures keeping perfect time.

With a rhythm that's fresh and bold,
The euphony of earth unfolds.
A playful symphony down below,
Where seeds and laughter freely grow.

Colors of the Quiet Dawn

The sun sneezed bright, sky turned a sneeze,
A rooster crowed, while the cat caught a breeze.
Colors juggled, like clowns in a show,
Morning winked, said 'Ready, set, go!'

Blueberries danced with rhubarb delight,
A pickle popped in, oh what a sight!
Jellybeans laughed, hung out on the green,
At dawn's party, they made quite a scene.

Pancakes flipped high, in the breeze took flight,
Maple syrup drizzled, glistening bright.
The grass wore sandals, all set for play,
In this morning circus, come join the fray!

So grab your hat, it's time to prance,
In colors of dawn, we'll shake our pants.
With giggles and glee, we'll dance till noon,
In the garden of jokes, underneath the moon.

Tapestry of Fragrance

Skunks wore suits, oh what a sight,
Perfumed petals took flight in the light.
A daisy told jokes, while roses just gloated,
Lavender laughed—'Why are we floated?'

Lilies stirred soup with a fragrant smile,
A hiccup from daisies echoed a mile.
Petunias painted, their hues were a splash,
As bees played poker, all hoping for cash.

A tulip tried limbo but fell in a pot,
While onion rings giggled, thinking they're hot.
With garlic as backup, they rocked the square,
In nature's playhouse, what fun we shared!

From soil to sky, aromas combined,
In this crazy quilt, joy and chaos aligned.
A riddle of scents—what potion is this?
In the tapestry of fragrance, we find our bliss!

Nature's Lyrical Revival

The wind picked up, blew onto a branch,
Where squirrels debated, 'Should we take a chance?'
The leaves started singing, a tuneful escape,
With chirps from the bluebirds—they all wore a cape!

Butterflies giggled, spun circles in air,
Twirled by the daisies, no worries or care.
A worm started rapping, all snug in its hole,
While frogs formed a band, oh what a stroll!

Grasshoppers breakdanced, with a boing and a hop,
All nature's creatures, non-stop on the bop.
Dandelions blew wishes like bubbles in glee,
'Goodbye to the lawnmower! Let's all be free!'

With rhythm and laughter, they danced and they played,
In the light of the sun, their worries delayed.
Nature's revival, a carnival scene,
Where joy is the anthem, and giggles convene!

The Essence of Petal Poetry

A rose wrote a sonnet, so witty and bold,
While a daffodil giggled, its rhyme was pure gold.
Magnolias strutted, with elegance rare,
Underneath them, the ants held a poetry fair.

The lilacs were buzzin' with tales of delight,
While petunias whispered, 'Let's dance through the night!'

With ink made of nectar, they penned with flair,
The essence of flowers, a whimsical air.

Pansies recited their verses with pride,
While bees brought the beats, oh what a ride!
A sunflower hosted, with grandeur and grace,
In a field of their dreams, they all found their place.

So let's take a moment, to laugh and to cheer,
For poetry rests in the wildflower's sphere.
In this garden of giggles, where merriment flows,
The essence of petals is laughter that grows!

The Language of Blossoms

Petals whisper secrets, oh so bright,
They giggle in colors, a true delight.
Dandelions dance in a silly parade,
While tulips make jokes in a sunbeam charade.

Bees wear tiny suits, buzzing with flair,
Roses choose puns, they show they care.
Buds laugh together, with pollen they play,
In this garden of giggles, who needs a bouquet?

Silly sunflowers sway, heads held high,
Demanding the sun, while clouds pass by.
They nod 'yes!' to jokes that make them sway,
In the language of blossoms, a frolicsome ballet.

So join in the fun, as nature's in rhyme,
With each little blossom, we laugh every time.
In this floral comedy, let joy be the goal,
Where every bloom's joke tickles the soul.

Heartbeats Beneath the Soil

Underground whispers, roots tickle and tease,
Earthworms are giggling, just doing as they please.
They throw soil parties, with mud pies on trays,
In their cozy burrows, they dance and they play.

Beets wear their capes, like veggies in flight,
They dodge the potatoes, it's quite a sight!
Meanwhile, the carrots giggle underground,
With a punchline so funny, it shakes the brown mound.

The radishes root for their veggie parade,
While grasses crack jokes, the lawn's well displayed.
In this playful realm, beneath all the fuss,
They laugh at the daisies, who feel quite a plus.

So remember, dear friend, while life seems so tough,
There's laughter below where it's all just enough.
In this rhythm of life, with heartbeats in clay,
The soil holds our dreams, in the silliest way.

A Stanza of Spring

Spring wakes up yawning, stretching in bed,
With socks made of petals and a hat on its head.
Raindrops are laughing, they slide down the eaves,
While frogs croak out verses, composing spring leaves.

The daisies are poets, reciting their lines,
With tulips as audience, sipping on wines.
They gather for tea, in the soft morning glow,
In a tale full of nature, the fun starts to flow.

Birds chirp a chorus, with tunes that amuse,
Their tweets filled with humor, no chance to snooze.
Butterflies flutter, with costumes so bright,
They twist and they twirl, in sheer pure delight.

So come on, my friend, to this stanza of cheer,
Where each flower sings, and the laughter is near.
In a springtime melody, every petal will bring,
A sonnet of joy that will make your heart sing.

Scrolls of Sun-kissed Meadows

In meadows so sunny, where daisies unite,
They share old scrolls, making jokes out of light.
Buttercups giggle at shadows that sway,
While laughter unfurls in the breezy bouquets.

Silly grasses gossip, each blade has a tale,
About chubby little snails, slow hoping to sail.
They roll out the scrolls, with punchlines so grand,
As they weave through the wildflowers, hand in hand.

The wind writes a poem, a whimsical tune,
Tickling the petals, beneath the bright moon.
Sun-kissed, they sway, in a dance that inspires,
Every meadow a stage, igniting our desires.

So join the fun, in this scroll-wrapped delight,
Where laughs grow like flowers, in the soft warm light.
In these fields of humor, let your heart soar,
For sun-kissed meadows hold laughter galore.

Rhymes in the Rose

In the garden, roses flirt,
Wearing skirts of crimson shirt.
They giggle in the morning light,
Dancing with the bees in flight.

A daisy dashes, 'I'm the star!'
But thorns are here, they raise the bar.
The petals whisper, 'What a show!'
A rosy blush, with cheeky glow.

Along comes tulip, bold and bright,
"Oh please, my colors are a sight!"
But roses just roll their eyes,
"Petals, you've got quite the size!"

Yet in this patch of leafy cheer,
All flowers laugh, no room for fear.
With every joke, the sun beams wide,
In nature's giggle, we all abide.

The Garden's Gaze

In the garden, sunflowers peek,
"Hey look at me! I'm quite unique!"
They turn their heads to catch the sun,
While tulips giggle, "Oh what fun!"

The daisies whisper half a plot,
"Told that bee he's not so hot!"
But bees just buzz and join the fray,
Creating joy throughout the day.

With every wave and breezy dance,
The petals twirl in sheer romance.
The leaves declare in mighty cheer,
"Let's host a ball—everyone's here!"

But roses grumble, "Where's our throne?"
The lilacs laugh, "You're not alone!"
In this garden's cheeky play,
All blooms unite, come what may.

Unruly Petals

Oh, the petals with their sass,
Throwing color, brassy class.
The marigolds shout, "We run this place!"
While daisies try to keep up pace.

The poppies puff with bold delight,
"Who needs rules? We'll take a bite!"
Their leafy friends just roll their eyes,
"More chaos? Oh, what a surprise!"

With every breeze, the troubles grow,
They tumble down, put on a show.
"Let's take a selfie!" giggles bloom,
In petals wild, they find their room.

But with the moon, they sense the calm,
Under stars, they hum a psalm.
These unruly petals, wild and free,
Find peace in laughter, that's the key.

Secret Life of Stems

What secrets lie beneath the ground?
Those stems are whispering all around.
"Did you hear what that rose said?"
"Last night, he slept—without his head!"

The daisies laugh, they share a tale,
Of sneaky roots who go to gale.
The stems all wiggle, oh what fun,
"Who knew we'd let our humor run?"

When winds come calling, they just twirl,
"Hold on tight, let's give it a whirl!"
In the garden theater, flowers play,
As stems keep secrets, day by day.

So if you wonder what they say,
In breezy nights or sunlit day,
Just listen close, enjoy the tune,
In nature's world, there's always room.

Secrets in the Petal's Fold

A little bug with a funky hat,
Danced on a leaf, in love with a cat.
They giggled together, oh what a sight,
As daisies erupted in laughter at night.

Petals confided in winds that blew,
Sharing their tales of morning dew.
The bees started chuckling, buzzed with glee,
While butterflies waltzed, so fancy and free.

In shadows of leaves, secrets unfold,
Whispers of nature, daring and bold.
Stems try to tickle, but they trip and fall,
A riot in gardens, giggles through all.

At twilight's curtain, a party is thrown,
With crickets as DJs, excitement is grown.
The petals bow down - what an uproar!
A funny affair that we all adore!

Rhythms in the Wildflower

In fields of color, wildflowers sway,
Doing the cha-cha, come join the fray.
A sunflower twirled, but lost her cap,
The daisies all snickered, a hilarious trap.

A bee declared, "Let's start a band!"
A ladybug played drums, all unplanned.
They jammed till the moon said, "Not so fast!"
But the laughter of petals echoed, unsurpassed.

The roses blushed, tried to join in,
But tangled their thorns, oh where to begin?
A tulip with grace leapt over the vines,
While a clumsy old weed said, "Hey, check my lines!"

Through rhythm and giggles, the evening flew,
With blossoms that danced, in a colorful crew.
Each stem had a joke, the laughter was grand,
In wildflower worlds, where mischief is planned!

Blooms Beneath the Sky

Up in the sky, the clouds made a fuss,
A flower asked why they were in such a rush.
The sun winked down, "You know it's all fun,
When blooms reach high, just to tickle the sun!"

A dandelion puff with a giggly grin,
Declared, "Let's float! Let the games begin!"
As petals blew kisses on breezes so wild,
The sky got all bashful, like a shy child.

With laughter like raindrops, the blossoms all sang,
While clusters of pollen began doing the clang.
The clouds danced along, in a fluffy ballet,
As nature's chorus held court for the day.

At twilight's curtain, the stars came to play,
To twinkle and tease in their sparkly way.
The blooms waved goodbye, all weary, yet spry,
For tomorrow they'd giggle beneath the same sky.

Harmony of Garden Spirits

In a garden so quirky, spirits did rhyme,
They danced with the daisies, lost track of time.
A gnarled old root told a tall tale with flair,
While worms in the soil snorted, "Oh, please, share!"

The roses wore crowns made of thorns and delight,
With grasshoppers crooning till the edge of night.
A whimsical wind spread the laughter so wide,
It tickled the petals, they giggled and cried.

A foxglove in polka dots led the parade,
With a wobbly stem, just a bit mislaid.
"Come join us, good friends, we're all quite absurd,
In this garden of chaos, hearts fly like a bird!"

As the moon cast a glow, the spirits took flight,
Spinning tales of magic, in the soft silver light.
In harmony's rhythm, the garden ignites,
A symphony blooms under starry delights!

In the Shade of Lilacs

Sitting 'neath the lilacs' flair,
I found a frog with purple hair.
He croaked a tune, a silly song,
And danced along—the joke was long.

A bee zoomed past with quite a buzz,
It paused to say, "You look like fuzz!"
I laughed so hard, I nearly cried,
The lilacs giggled; I sighed with pride.

The flowers whispered, "What's the tea?"
"I think that bee just stole my key!"
We spun around; the breeze was sweet,
In lilac's shade, no room for defeat.

So if you're feeling down and low,
Just find a lilac; let it show.
With jokes and fun, they'll lift your heart,
In their sweet shade, we'll never part.

Awakened by the Dawn

The rooster crowed—a bird in jest,
Said, "Morning folks, it's time for rest!"
I tumbled out of bed with style,
Still dreaming of my cozy pile.

A sunbeam peeked right through the blinds,
It tickled my nose and crossed my mind.
"Get up, you sleepy little chip!"
I swayed too long, and took a dip.

The kettle sang a merry tune,
As I danced 'round with a broom at noon.
The cat just sighed and rolled her eyes,
This morning dance was quite a surprise!

So if you rise with a sleepy frown,
Just join the fun; don't let it drown.
Life's too short for morning gloom,
Let laughter bloom within each room.

The Blossom's Dance

Petals twirled in the gentle breeze,
They spun around like clumsy bees.
"Watch my moves!" a tulip called,
We cheered him on as he appalled.

A daffodil slipped, oh what a sight!
He flopped and flailed with all his might.
The daisies giggled, swaying tall,
Together we danced; we gave it our all.

"Come join us, friend!" a rose did shout,
"Bring your quirks, there's room to spout!"
The sky lit up—an audience in bloom,
As we laughed and spun, filling the room.

So join the dance, let laughter flow,
Embrace the quirks; let your spirit glow.
In every step, joy does enhance,
Together we'll waltz—our silly dance!

Vibrant Verses

In a garden where squirrels debate,
I penned my thoughts—what a great fate!
A tulip peeped, "What's that you wrote?"
"Just a silly line about a goat!"

A butterfly flitted with a grin,
"Make room for me, let the fun begin!"
He spun around, causing a ruckus,
A hiccup here, a friendly fuss!

Each petal cheered, each leaf clapped loud,
We created verses, funny and proud.
"More puns, more giggles, let them collide!"
In this vibrant space, we all confide.

So gather 'round, let humor rain,
In vibrant verses, we'll entertain.
With laughter and joy, we'll write our way,
Through this delightful, silly play!

Petals in the Wind

Petals dance like clumsy clowns,
Tumbling through the sleepy towns.
They swirl around in a silly race,
Chasing bees at a comical pace.

A flower sneezes, pollen flies,
Bees wear hats and start to cry.
They bump their heads on daffodil bows,
While the sun giggles, oh how it glows!

Colors clash like socks unpaired,
Even the daisies look quite scared.
With every turn, they twist and shout,
The garden's thrumming with laughs, no doubt!

So if you see the petals caper,
Join the fun, grab a paper,
Let's write the tales of silly things,
In a world where every flower sings!

Secrets of the Springtime

In spring, the ants wear tiny hats,
They strut around like fancy brats.
With cookie crumbs held up high,
They march along, oh my, oh my!

The tulips gossip, what a scene!
About the rose who wears too green.
They roll their petals, laugh and play,
Trying to outshine the sunny day.

Even the frogs have catchy tunes,
They sing and dance beneath the moons.
"You think you're great?" a squirrel chimes,
"Just wait for us; we're full of rhymes!"

The secrets bloom in giggles bright,
As flowers play their springtime flight.
Join in the laughter, come on, scoot!
Let's dance alongside this funny root!

Echoes of Fragrant Dreams

In gardens where the scents collide,
The daisies brag, they won't subside.
"I smell of sunshine, what about you?"
Said lavender, with a scent so true.

The roses joke, their petals lush,
"Ever tried a leafy crush?"
While violets giggle, light and sweet,
And dandelions tumble on their feet.

A bumblebee buzzes, quite bemused,
With all these flowers, I'm a bit confused!
They chime and chortle, their laughter booms,
In a fragrant land where joy resumes.

Echoes of cheer fill every breeze,
As blossoms dance with swaggered ease.
Come join the fun, no need for schemes,
Let's waltz in echoes of fragrant dreams!

Whispers Among the Lilies

Underneath the lilies, whispers spin,
Of frogs who think they're ninjas, kin.
They leap and land with clumsy flair,
While dragonflies twist in the air.

"Can you see me?" a lily pad grins,
"I'll vanish fast, just watch my spins!"
The ducks giggle, bobbing along,
In this flowered place where all belong.

"Well, I'm a flower of exquisite grace,"
Said the tulip, striking a pose with face.
But the wind laughed, and whoosh, off it went,
Leaving the tulip quite outspent!

So join the whispers, enjoy the play,
As lilies share secrets in their sway.
With goofy grins, they twirl and peek,
In this lively world, no need to be meek!

Garden of Verses

In the garden where tomatoes play,
They wear their red coats every day.
The carrots giggle, buried in dirt,
While silly peas jump in their green skirt.

The daisies dance with the bumblebee,
But watch out for pollen, it's quite sneezy!
A sunflower poses, tall and proud,
While the weeds whisper jokes, quite loud.

Roses say, 'We're the best in town!'
But dandelions are just rolling around.
The cucumbers pickle their funny jokes,
As everyone laughs, not one folksy hoax.

So come take a stroll through this patch so bright,
Where veggies and flowers share pure delight.
With giggles and grins, it's a sight to behold,
In this garden of verses, laughter unfolds.

The Dance of Blossoms

The tulips twirl in a breezy spin,
While violets chuckle, they're set to win.
A daffodil dips, then leaps with glee,
Shouting, 'Look at me! I'm a dancing spree!'

A bumblebee buzzes, 'Let's start a show!'
The petals join in, with a vibrant glow.
While pansies snicker, 'This is our night!'
As ladybugs tango under moonlight.

The roses take turns, telling old jokes,
While marigolds giggle, both sly and folks.
'What did one flower say to the sun?'
'You light up my life, isn't that fun?'

In this merry dance, all tensions cease,
With blossoms united, there's purest peace.
So twirl with us, in this floral display,
A rhythmic fiesta, hooray, hooray!

Nature's Poetic Palette

In nature's canvas, colors collide,
With splashes of laughter, not a moment to hide.
The orange tulips sneak a sly peek,
While the bluebells giggle, they're quite a freak.

The sunflowers wear shades, quite the trend,
Laughing together, they blend and mend.
While the lilacs whisper, 'Is it time for tea?'
And the daisies respond, 'Oh, just wait for me!'

Oh, what a ruckus, under the moon,
As paint-splattered petals coo a sweet tune.
Each stroke a chuckle, each hue a jest,
In this vibrant masterpiece, we're endlessly blessed.

So let's join in, paint laughter anew,
With a brush of joy and a compliment too.
In nature's palette, we dance and we sing,
For life's a canvas that blooms every spring.

Symphony of Flowering Hearts

In the meadow, where daisies strum,
A symphony plays, and oh, it's fun!
The wind is a maestro, waving his wand,
While the clovers join in, a charming band.

The roses sing of love and cheer,
With a pitch so sweet, they draw you near.
But lilies laugh loud, 'What's love got to do?'
And the orchids whisper, 'Let's dance and woo!'

A chorus of laughter, blossoms unite,
While the pansies flash winks, pure delight.
With beetles as dancers, and crickets a'play,
The heartstrings of flowers bring joy to the day.

So gather 'round, let your worries part,
Join this delightful symphony of heart.
In the garden of giggles, we'll let love start,
As we sway with the petals, a magical art!

The Narrative of Nectar

In a garden of sweet desire,
Honey bees dream of being higher.
They dance in circles, oh what a sight,
Passing juice in pure delight.

Flowers giggle at the clumsy flight,
While ants march on, their armor tight.
'Is that pollen on your shoe?'
'No, that's breakfast, want some too?'

The butterflies wear their finest lace,
Flaunting colors, oh what a race!
They bump and tumble, what a fuss,
But laughter rings, no need to rush.

At sunset, the garden sighs,
Underneath the starry skies.
Sipping nectar, sipping dreams,
In this realm where nothing's as it seems.

Garden of Dreams

In the garden where veggies chat,
A radish said, 'I'm quite the brat.'
Tomatoes blushed from tales of doom,
As carrots giggled in their bloom.

The squash declares, 'I'm quite the catch!'
With puns that make the leeks all hatch.
'Zucchini's on a tiny spree,
Wearing stripes, just like me!'

At the dance, the herbs all spin,
Basil twirls with parsley, a win!
Chives are snickering in delight,
While mint teases, 'You smell just right!'

And when the sun begins to fade,
In laughter shared, the night's portrayed.
In this patch where nonsense flows,
The garden dreams, and laughter grows.

The Symphony of Flora

Cacti strum their prickly strings,
While daisies hum of sunny things.
A dandelion serenade,
While butterflies join in the parade.

The roses boast of rich perfume,
While pollen-filled bees vroom vroom.
Fir trees tap their woody feet,
As vines appear to sway, oh sweet!

A peony winks, its petals wide,
'Come dance with me!' it bellowed with pride.
But oh, the tulips trip and fall,
Creating laughter across the hall.

Together they'll sing till late,
With all the blooms, they celebrate.
In this symphony of grassy dreams,
Where fun and flowers sprout in beams.

Whispers among the Wisps

In shadows where the wild things giggle,
The fireflies plot their nightly wiggle.
'Don't blink!' says one with a grin,
'We might disappear and then come in!'

The mushrooms whisper tales of night,
'What if we dressed in shades of bright?'
While brambles conspire to intertwine,
Unraveling plans in sweet sunshine.

Cumulus clouds, fluffy and spry,
Spin stories of laughter in the sky.
But watch out for raindrops, oh so sly,
They'll giggle and tumble, oh my, oh my!

So let the whimsy grow wild and free,
With laughter linked to a nearest tree.
In whispers soft, the garden thrives,
Where humor and nature are simply alive.

Ode to Gardeners

With trowel in hand, they dig with glee,
Their plants won't grow if they drink too much tea.
The worms all wiggle, they dance and sway,
While the weeds hold a party, just down the way.

Gardeners gossip, with spades held high,
About the tomatoes that touch the sky.
"Too much sun, or too much rain?"
They chuckle as the snails join the train.

When herbs start to speak in rhymes so sweet,
They argue with carrots on who's the best treat.
But when salad bowls come, it's all in vain,
For they all end up in a crunchy domain.

In hats of green, under sun's bright glow,
They prance around like they own the show.
With clumps of dirt stuck high on their shoes,
These silly gardeners have nothing to lose!

The Scent of Stanzas

In fields of words, the flowers grow,
Each petal a line, with rhythm in tow.
Bees buzz along, with a poetic sting,
While butterflies laugh at the verse they bring.

A daisy claims it's the star of the verse,
While roses argue, "No, that's a curse!"
Tulips take sides, with laughter they shout,
As violets giggle, "What's it all about?"

Pansies paint pictures in colors so bold,
While sunflowers boast of the stories they've told.
A sunbeam smiles, lighting up the scene,
As petals do a dance, all fresh and green.

The scent of stanzas fills the air,
With lines that tickle, and teasing flair.
In this garden of verses, we find our cheer,
Where laughter blooms, and joy is near!

Petal-sweet Harmony

A choir of petals sings soft and low,
In gardens where giggles and breezes flow.
With bees as conductors, they harmonize bright,
While the sun shines red, telling jokes in the light.

Daisies whisper secrets, odes of the morn,
As tulips shout, "Hey, we were just born!"
The daisies retort with their innocent charm,
"Your loudness is cute, but we're still the calm!"

Through laughter and fragrance, they form a band,
With daisies a-dancing—oh, isn't it grand?
The garden's alive with a melody sweet,
As petals keep rhythm, with accents discreet.

Petal-sweet vibes fill the sun-kissed air,
With flowers all giggling, with fluff in their hair.
In this world of green, where humor blooms wide,
The harmony's laughter is the petal's pride.

Nature's Tender Lyrics

Nature writes verses in green and brown,
With squirrels in hats and a scarecrow crown.
The wind hums a tune as the flowers sway,
While raindrops tap dance, to chase gloom away.

A robin sings sonnets in the morning sun,
With worms as his backup, they have so much fun!
While crickets compose under moon's gentle gaze,
They laugh at the frogs as they croak their praise.

In a waltz of petals, the dance goes on,
With blossoms and grasses, they sway till dawn.
From daisies to lilies, they prance so free,
Cracking up everyone, even the bee!

Nature's lyrics flow with a playful beat,
In gardens where laughter and flowers meet.
So let's join the chorus, and dance in delight,
For in this wild concert, all feels just right!

Floral Dreams

In a garden where daisies act how they please,
Tulips wear hats made of fresh summer breeze.
The sun laughs out loud, tickling bees,
While roses compete in their fanciest tease.

Pansies gossip about their bright hues,
While sunflowers dress in their tallest shoes.
A dandy hare hops, causing quite a ruse,
Chasing scents of the morning dew muse.

Butterflies flutter, with tales of their flights,
Trading secrets with glowworms on nights.
They dance with the stars as they sip on delights,
And giggle at squirrels with acorn-filled sights.

In this realm of laughter, oh what a sight,
Where petunias prance and forget all their fright.
Here, joy blooms freely, a pure delight,
A floral tango under the moonlight.

Sonnet of the Seasons

Spring sings a tune in a vibrant parade,
While winter chuckles at the socks that you've made.
Summer's a joker, in flip-flops displayed,
And autumn drops leaves, like confetti, unafraid.

Dandelions giggle as they take to the air,
With wishes and dreams, oh, they don't have a care.
The frost tickles petals, a hilarious dare,
As crocus and lily join the fanciful affair.

Clouds in the sky wear their fluffiest grins,
Playing games with the sun, as the day spins.
In seasons of jest, everyone wins,
A riot of colors, where laughter begins.

So let's dance with the flowers, let worries unbind,
For in this wild garden, pure joy we will find.
Each petal a giggle, each stem intertwined,
A sonnet of seasons with laughter aligned.

Garden of Verses

In a garden of rhymes where the daffodils play,
The marigolds chuckle at clouds that delay.
"Why hurry!" they chime, "Let us laugh, come what may!"
While the violets giggle, all decked out in sway.

Bees hum a tune as they dance on the breeze,
Bumbling around like they're stuck in the trees.
With petals as couches, they lounge as they please,
Tickled by whispers of flowers at ease.

There's a fern in the corner who tells silly tales,
Of sneaky old snails and their dodgy sales.
Amidst the wild blooms where laughter prevails,
A world where the humor forever inhales.

So come to this garden, bring giggles and cheer,
Among plants full of charm, nothing to fear.
Each verse has its story, from far and near,
In this jolly patch where all laughter is clear.

The Symphony of Blooms

In the garden, a symphony plays with a grin,
Where petals dance lightly and laughter begins.
The orchids conduct with their vibrant skin,
While pansies perform in their fanciest spins.

Daisies parade in their polka-dot clothes,
And lilacs hum sweetly, the audience glows.
The sun enters stage left, and everyone knows,
A concert of giggles where everyone grows.

Carrots take solos with marvelous flair,
Rhythmic beetroot joins in, without a care.
The trumpet of tulips fills up the air,
While a peacock struts by, causing stares everywhere.

So gather your friends, bring joy to the stream,
For the flowers are ready, it's time to redeem.
In this symphony of blooms, let laughter beam,
A playful production, a wonderful dream.

Divergence of Daisy Lines

In a field of daisies, one thought it cool,
To wear a hat, like a goofy jewel.
But the wind had its say, blew it off with glee,
Now the daisy's just bare, oh what a sight to see!

Butterflies chuckled, while snacking on cake,
'Is that daisy a comedian, or just a mistake?'
With petals all ruffled, it told them a joke,
You should see my old outfit, it really was bespoke!

The bees joined in laughing, buzzing near the stem,
'That hat was too big, we'd never wear them!'
But the daisy just grinned, said, 'Fashion's a breeze,
Except when it's windy, then style's hard to seize!'

So they danced in the grass, with laughter so bright,
Playing tag with the clouds, what a silly sight!
In a world full of petals, where silliness thrives,
You'll always find humor, in blooming lives!

The Lyrical Leaf

A leaf in the breeze, played a tune with delight,
It danced like a fool, in the morning light.
Said, 'Look at me twirl, I'm a star in this show,
But watch out for squirrels, they steal my limbo flow!'

The branches all cheered, what a raucous affair!
While the sun burst with laughter, causing leaves to bare.
They giggled together, what a sight to behold,
As the wind played the flute, and the trees sang bold!

A squirrel took a bow, said, 'I want in this game!'
But he slipped on a nut, and oh what a shame!
The leaf rolled with laughter, spun round and around,
'You'll need better shoes, before you tumble down!'

So the leaf flew high, it waved at the sky,
Sending silly greetings, to the clouds up high.
In a dance of joy, they all swayed and swirled,
For in trees and in laughter, a universe twirled!

Tones of the Tulip

A tulip stood tall, with colors so bright,
Claimed it was the best, oh what a sight!
But a passing rose said, with a cheeky grin,
'Look at those petals, where do we begin?'

'That shade of pink is well, just so last year!'
The tulip did huff, 'That's so insincere!'
They bickered all day, about floral finesse,
While bees kept chuckling, in pure happiness.

'Tulips can't dance, they just wiggle and sway,'
The daisies piped up, in their charming way.
'But we can sing ballads, and hum out of tune,
While wearing fine hats made of marshmallow moon!'

In a garden of giggles, they came to a truce,
To create a new trend, as they rallied for juice.
With petals all rustling, they laughed at the night,
In a riot of colors, everything felt right!

Cadence of the Cosmos

A moonbeam was rapping, to stars in the sky,
Said, 'Check out my moves, I'm a cosmic guy!'
The planets all laughed, at the lunar fanfare,
Said, 'You dance like a comet, all over the air!'

The sun joined the party, in a fiery suit,
Swirling around, in a bright golden toot.
While asteroids chimed in, with clinks and with clatters,
Each one told a story, of interstellar matters.

While comets wiggled, and danced in a row,
They shimmied and giggled, 'We're putting on a show!'
The Milky Way twinkled, with laughter in streams,
As the universe swayed, in their night-time dreams!

A black hole laughed loud, 'I'll just pull you all in!'
But the stars shone back bright, 'You won't beat our grin!'

In the cadence of cosmos, they found joyful plays,
Creating funny moments, in the vastness of rays!

Lyrics in Full Bloom

In the garden of words, I trip,
Over sentences that dance and skip.
They giggle and laugh, such silly sights,
As they twirl around like kites in flights.

A sunflower whispers to a rose,
"Why do you wear such a fancy nose?"
The daffodils chuckle, sharing a joke,
While daisies play hopscotch on a yoke.

The tulips stand straight, puffed with pride,
But the weeds just laugh from the side.
A butterfly winks, it's quite the show,
While a gnome munches popcorn, watching the flow.

Oh, the petals speak in rhymes and laughter,
Creating verses that chase happily ever after.
In this garden of giggles, let's all pretend,
That each little poem is a fun, leafy friend.

Canopy of Colors

Under a sky of vibrant hues,
There's a plant that wears mismatched shoes.
It hops to the left and then to the right,
Singing songs of a wild delight.

The daisies throw a vibrant parade,
While hyacinths join, all dressed and made.
They spin and they swirl in a colorful whirl,
While butterflies giggle, giving a twirl.

A tree offers shade, with a wink and a nod,
Saying, "Come dance, you silly little sod!"
The petals tumble, each has a scheme,
In this canopy colors weave through a dream.

Oh, the laughter that flows from root to bloom,
With every little giggle, there's always more room.
Join the fun, let's brighten the day,
In this garden of joy, come out and play!

The Poetry of Petal Paths

In a maze made of petals, let's take a stroll,
With rhymes to discover, poetry's goal.
A lily sings low, a sweet, silly tune,
While daisies hold hands and dance 'neath the moon.

A bumblebee buzzes, and trips on a rhyme,
Saying, "Did you hear that? I'm out of time!"
The ladybugs giggle, rolling on leaves,
As poems emerge like fresh blooming sheaves.

In this path of petals, laughter is key,
Each step a new verse, come stroll along with me.
The roses tease violets, growing so tall,
While daisies gently whisper, "Let's all have a ball!"

The poetry flows like a lively parade,
With each little petal, a joyful escapade.
Let's dance through this garden, let giggles combine,
In the path of silly verses, it's all quite divine.

Rhyme of Radiance

In a field where the sillies begin to play,
Radiant flowers giggle the day away.
Petunias wear hats, quite out of style,
As they strut their stuff with a cheeky smile.

The daisies debate the best kind of hair,
While sunflowers gossip, no worries, no care.
A zany dance-off breaks out on the green,
With pollen confetti bursting the scene.

The bees bring the beats, oh, what a sound,
With each buzz and flutter, pure joy is found.
In the rhyme of radiance, fun takes the lead,
As each little flower plants laughter's seed.

So come join the fun, let your worries all fade,
In this whimsical garden, where laughter is made.
With flowers and friends, let's create a grand show,
In the rhyme of radiance, let hilarity grow!

www.ingramcontent.com/pod-product-compliance
Lightning Source LLC
Chambersburg PA
CBHW071823160426
43209CB00003B/181